Watch Me Build a Sandcastle

By Jack Otten

Children's Press®
A Division of Scholastic Inc.
New York / Toronto / London / Auckland / Sydney
Mexico City / New Delhi / Hong Kong
Danbury, Connecticut

Photo Credits: Cover and all photos by Maura Boruchow
Contributing Editor: Jennifer Silate
Book Design: Michelle Innes

Library of Congress Cataloging-in-Publication Data

Otten, Jack.
Watch me build a sandcastle / by Jack Otten.
    p. cm. -- (Making things)
Includes index.
Summary: A young boy demonstrates how he uses a bucket shaped
like a castle, sea shells, and sand to build his sandcastle.
   ISBN 0-516-23946-5 (lib. bdg.) -- ISBN 0-516-23496-X (pbk.)
    1. Sand craft--Juvenile literature. 2. Sandcastles--Juvenile literature.
    [1. Sand craft. 2. Handicraft. 3. Sandcastles.] I. Title.

TT865 .O88 2002
731.4'5--dc21
                                                      2001037279

Contents

My name is Jim.

I like to play in the sand at the **beach**.

The beach is a good place to build a **sandcastle**.

First, I put wet sand in my **pail**.

I fill my pail to the top.

I pack the sand in tightly.

Next, I slowly turn the pail over.

I'm careful not to let any sand spill out.

I lift the pail.

The wet sand stays in the shape of the pail.

Next, I use my finger to draw a door on my sandcastle.

I put **shells** around my sandcastle.

They make it look nice.

17

Then, I make a wall around my sandcastle.

I pat the sand with my hands.

I make the wall high.

19

Do you like my sandcastle?

20

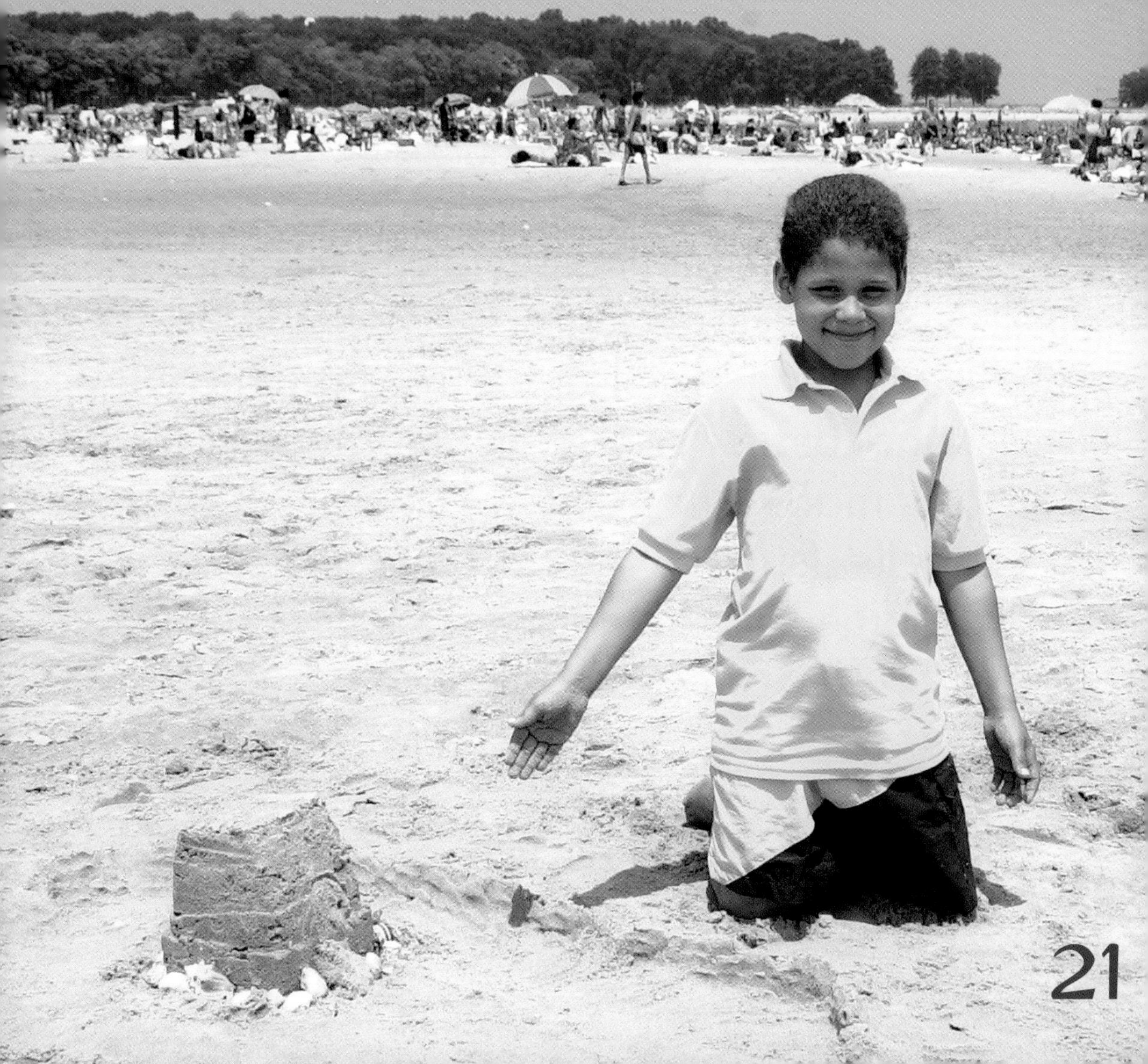

New Words

beach (**beech**) sandy land by a sea, ocean, or river

pail (**payl**) a container to put things in

sandcastle (**sand-cas**-uhl) a castle that is made out of sand

shells (**shehlz**) the hard coverings of some sea animals

To Find Out More

Books

Sandcastle
by Mick Inkpen
Harcourt Brace & Company

Super Sand Castle Saturday
by Stuart J. Murphy
HarperCollins Children's Books

Web Site
Sand Castle Central
http://www.sandcastlecentral.com
Learn all about sandcastles on this Web site.

Index

About the Author
Jack Otten is an author and educator living in New York City.

Reading Consultants
Kris Flynn, Coordinator, Small School District Literacy, The San Diego County Office of Education

Shelly Forys, Certified Reading Recovery Specialist, W.J. Zahnow Elementary School, Waterloo, IL

Sue McAdams, Former President of the North Texas Reading Council of the IRA, and Early Literacy Consultant, Dallas, TX